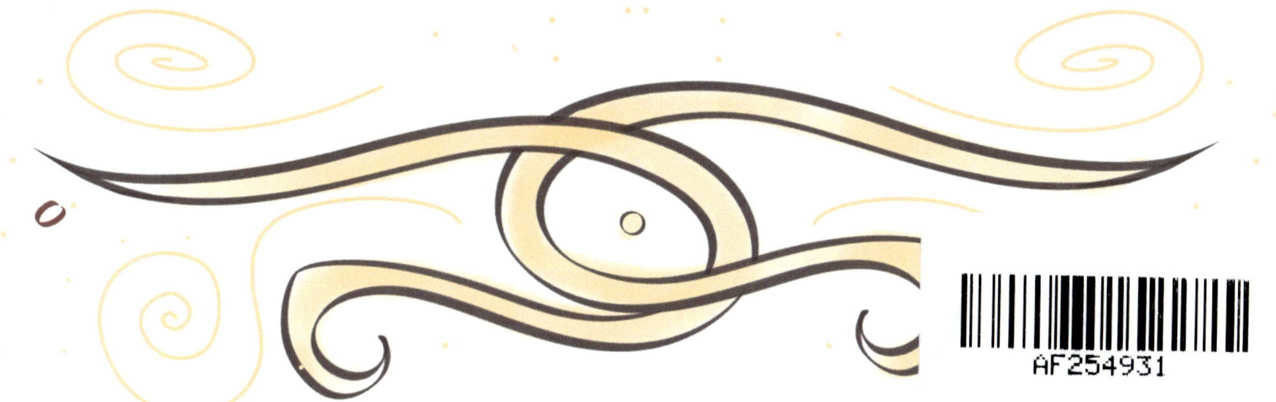

What Makes a Dancer?

by Christina Marlett

Illustrated by Mykola Gyryluk

Artis
PRESS

ISBN: 978-1-9994721-8-4

Published in Canada in 2022 by
Artis Press
Calgary, Alberta
www.artispress.ca

Designed by Artis Press.
Printed and bound by Amazon.

For my parents
who put me into dance lessons

What makes a dancer?

Let's **explore**

Practice ten years?

Maybe more?

Is it someone who dresses in
tutus and lace?
Someone with makeup
All over her face?

Do dancers have to know
All the right moves?
A B-Boy who **poses**,
pops, **locks** and **grooves**?

Maybe a dancer has special feet
that **Tip Tap** and **Clap** out
a special beat...

Maybe dancers can only be girls
who **balance** on tip toe
Spin dozens of twirls...

Maybe dancers
must dance in twos
Guiding, striding
to music they choose...

Maybe a dancer
must stay on beat
Matching music he hears
to rhythm of feet...

Or...

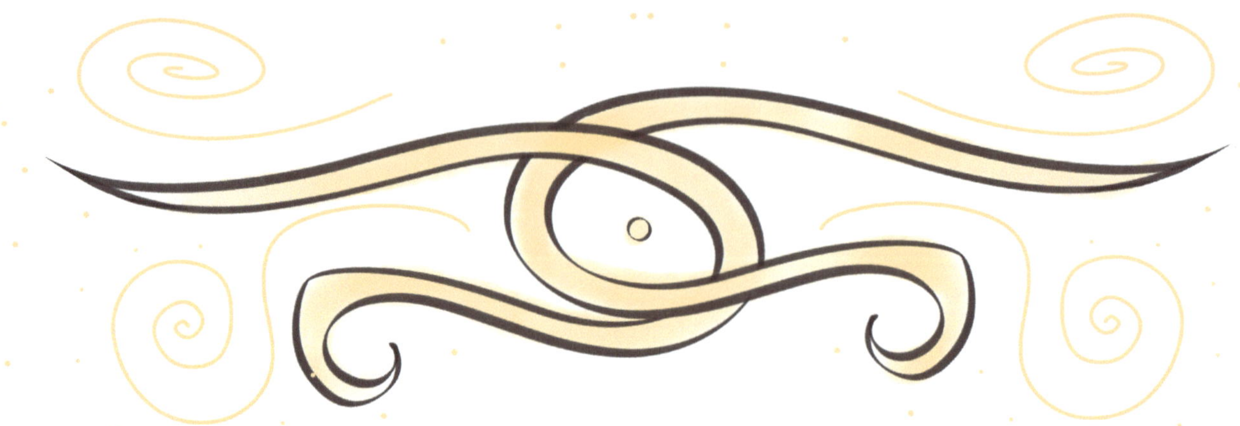

Maybe the dancers are **you** and **me**
and **dancing** is one way
We can be **free**

Our hearts beat the rhythm

We dance from within

Our movements unplanned

We **jump, glide** and **spin**

Dancing is **sacred**
Dancing is **fun**
When dancing together
Our hearts **beat** as one

Dance makes us **happy**
increasing **vibration**
boosting our energy
with **joyful** creation

If each human being
danced **every** day
The world would be **different**
We'd all find our way

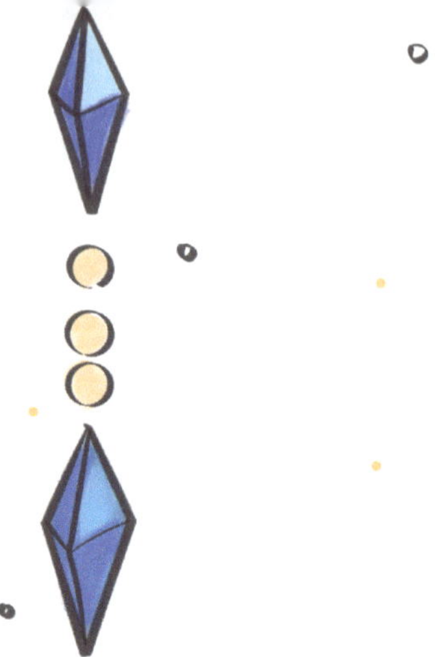

Because dance is expression
of **greatness** inside
When we share that with others
Our hearts **open** wide

So dance with me now—
Let's do our part
When we **show** others how
our **healing** can start

Dance with me now
It's our time to **shine**
to **pulsate**, to **gyrate**
Expressing divine

About the Dances

Ballet

The first ballet performances started a very long time ago in Italy. It was a dance for kings, queens and people who lived in the castles. Dance masters would teach the steps; music was played, and people danced for fun. Later, ballet spread to France, Russia and then all around the world. It's a very popular dance style for children, women and men that emphasizes grace, strength, flexibility and power. Ballet dance can be a way to tell stories like Cinderella and the Nutcracker, or it can be a medium for dancers to perform beautiful movement to music.

Jazz

You can't have jazz dance without jazz music. Both jazz music and jazz dance were brought to America by enslaved Africans. They danced as a way to keep their memories of home alive. It was such an exciting dance style that it spread quickly. There are so many styles of jazz dance. Some styles have funny names like the Cakewalk, Boogie Woogie, Jitterbug and Lindy Hop.

Hip Hop

Hip hop isn't just a dance style; it's a whole culture. It started in Black and Latino communities in the 1970s in New York City. Life in those communities was really hard, especially for young people.

Hip means present and Hop means action, so Hip Hop is a movement that represents freedom to grow, create and learn. The youth found a different way to express themselves through original movement, music, respect and community.

There are many styles of Hip Hop. Breaking is one of the early styles where dancers battle each other with dance moves and originality instead of violence. Hip Hop dance has saved a lot of lives and now it's popular all over the world.

Tap

Tap dance comes from blending together several different dance styles. When slave owners took away their slaves' traditional percussion instruments, they used their bodies to make rhythms instead. People from England and Ireland had a style of dance that used wooden clogs on their feet. These two dance styles got combined into early tap dancing. Today, tap dancers wear shoes that have metal taps on the soles. They can make all sorts of cool sounds by moving their feet in different ways against the floor.

Flamenco

Flamenco dance is a very passionate dance style that has mysterious beginnings in India, Spain and the Middle East. There is lots of really fast hand clapping, and complicated hand, arm and foot movements. The women wear huge skirts that are part of the choreography. Flamenco guitar adds to the emotion of the performance. There is often stillness at the beginning of a song, and then the music and dance build together into an explosion of rhythm and steps.

Waltz

The Waltz is a partner dance that started in Germany, hundreds of years ago. It's very graceful, smooth and romantic. It's performed to classical music that has a beat of 1-2-3, 1-2-3. Couples seem to float actress the dance floor as they do spins and complicated steps that use their whole bodies. They really have to cooperate and listen to each other without talking.

Marinera

The Marinera is Peru's national dance. It has its roots in Spanish, African and Indigenous dance. It's a dance for couples where the woman uses her skirt and handkerchief to tease the man with her graceful movements. The Marinera dance is performed to guitar and drum music and it has different variations all over Peru.

Khon

Khon dance comes from Thailand. It's a very fancy style of dance where masks are worn and the dancers tell a story that comes from India. The performance is a combination of dance, elaborate costumes, singing and music. Only kings and queens used to get to see Khon dance, but now anyone can watch it. You can even see it on Youtube!

Samba

The Samba is a carnival street dance from Brazil. It's another style that comes from enslaved Africans who lived in Portugal. The costumes are really exciting with lots of feathers, sparkles and beads. Samba music is so much fun; you can't hear it without your body wanting to start shaking and wiggling to the beat.

Sufi Whirling

Sufi Whirling is a dance style that is easy and hard at the same time. It's easy because it only has one step. Sufi dancers spin around with one hand pointed toward the sky and the other pointed toward the earth. It's hard because the dancers spin for a really long time. They must get dizzy, but they don't fall down. Why do they spin for so long? It helps them feel deeply happy and connected to the divine.

Lion Dance

The lion is so important in Chinese culture that it has its own dance. It symbolizes power, wisdom and strength. The Lion Dance is one of the most important traditions in the Chinese New Year celebrations.

Two dancers dress up as a colorful lion and perform movements to bring good luck for the rest of the year. One dancer is the head and front legs and the other is the tail and the back legs. The music for the lion dance is very exciting and loud. It has drums, cymbals and gongs. The lion looks like it is scratching, shaking and licking its fur. It can be very funny! Other styles of Lion Dance have the lion jumping, leaping, rolling and wrestling.

Tinikling

Tinikling is a folk dance from the Philippines that uses two bamboo poles. Two people hold the poles at each end and they tap them on the ground and against each other to a steady rhythm.

While the bamboo gets tapped, dancers leap in and out of the space between the poles. They have to concentrate really hard to make sure their feet and ankles don't get trapped in the bamboo. It's a tricky dance that's very impressive to watch.

Bharatanatyam

Bharatanatyam is a very old dance that comes from India. It's a dance style that makes both the dancers and the audience feel and express the love of the divine. The dancers wear beautiful, colorful costumes. Bharatanatyam only used to be performed by women, but now men can do it too.

When the dance was first created, there were lots of people who couldn't read the sacred texts, so this style of dance helped those people learn without needing to read.

Hopak

The Hopak dance is also known as Cossack dancing and it comes from Russia and the Ukraine hundreds of years ago. Men would go off to battle and when they came home, if they were victorious, they would celebrate with exciting dance moves. Musicians and singers would gather around and perform songs that got faster and faster.

The dancers would keep up to the music with moves that told stories of their battles. They made up the dances as they went along and the energy built until the end of the dance, where they performed great leaps, fast spins, split jumps and deep squats. Hopak dancing is popular all over the world today and is known for its high energy and joyful celebration.

O'Tea

The O'Tea dance comes from Tahiti. If you can shake your hips really fast, this dance is for you. The dancers move in time to drums. Only men used to be allowed to do this dance, but now anyone can do it. The dancers wear long grass skirts to accentuate the movements, along with complicated headpieces. The O'Tea dance tells stories about daily life activities such as warfare, sailing, and nature.

About the Author

Christina Marlett

Christina Marlett (BKin, BMEd*) is the author of the international bestselling book *How Ugly Awkward Dancing Changes Everything*. She has taught dance to humans ranging from six months to ninety-three years (the babies were the scariest students until she realized they were thrilled to clap their hands endlessly).

Christina gives workshops and speaks all over North America on topics such as How to Dance a Book, How to Get More Energy (without caffeine) and How to Be Happy for No Reason. As a perpetual student of life and spirituality, she loves to inspire people to move their bodies with joy.

In slightly related news, she grew up competing in tap dance, met her husband in a university dance class where she was a bowling pin and he was a bowler, and together, they won a salsa competition (the dance kind, not the food kind).

Visit her website www.ChristinaMarlett.com to find out about her upcoming books (there are about 5 more in the works).

For a complimentary curated music playlist to accompany this book, go to: www.ChristinaMarlett.com/what-makes-a-dancer-playlist

Super secret bonus points for you if you can figure out what kind of degree a BMEd is.

About the Illustrator

Mykola Gyryluk

Born in 2007, Mykola Gyryluk is a neurodiverse and transgender artist, who is passionate about drawing and writing. This book was the first one they ever illustrated. They are very hopeful that their art will inspire and show other youths in their communities that there are opportunities waiting for them.